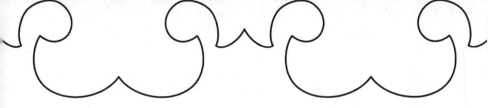

# Bulletin Boards
## for Christian Classrooms

Written by Carolyn Berg

Illustrated by Dan Farris

CONCORDIA PUBLISHING HOUSE • SAINT LOUIS

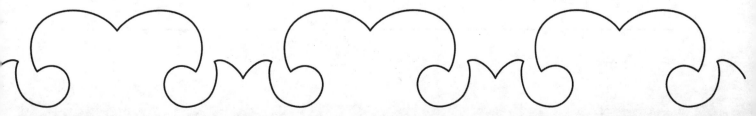

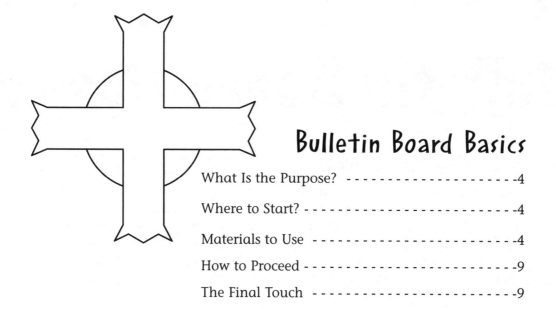

# Bulletin Board Basics

# Bulletin Board Ideas for the School Year
## Month-by-Month

# Patterns

# Bulletin Board Basics

## What Is the Purpose?

Is there such a thing as a "bulletin board" ministry? Absolutely. Throughout the history of mankind, God has given us avenues for sharing the promise of salvation. A message on a bulletin board may be a ray of hope to one in despair; it may be a signpost to lead a searching soul toward Christ; it may give the believer a deeper appreciation of God's love; it may give the unbeliever something to think about—maybe just enough to let the Holy Spirit begin His work.

As long as our messages are Christ-centered and based upon God's Holy Word, we can be sure they are effective: "My word ... goes out from My mouth: it will not return to Me empty, but will accomplish what I desire and achieve the purpose for which I sent it" (Isaiah 55:11).

## Where to Start?

These pages illustrate many ideas for getting started with Christian bulletin boards, yet this is just the beginning. Possible designs are nearly endless. However, when confronted with the task of preparing a bulletin board on a given topic or theme, there is only one place to start: "Take it to the Lord in prayer!" No task is ever too small or too large to ask for God's help.

Next, consider the location of the bulletin board. The message on a classroom bulletin board will be targeted to a specific group while a bulletin board located in a hallway in a school or church will have a broader audience. The designs offered in this book can be adapted to any location.

Then, consider the size of the bulletin board. You will need to adapt the designs suggested here to fit the space available to you. If you have access to an overhead projector, you can copy the patterns onto transparencies and then project them onto poster board to make patterns that are the correct size. A photocopier with an enlarging feature may be sufficient if you are working with a smaller space.

And finally, determine the materials you will use to create the bulletin board. The materials you choose depend on what is available and what you are comfortable working with. But also consider whether you will retain the elements of the bulletin board design to use again. If so, how you plan to store them will also influence the materials you choose to work with.

As you plan your bulletin boards, you will find the Lord leading you to certain passages of Scripture, reminding you of a meaningful line in a hymn or giving you a visual picture of a sermon or chapel talk. He will always find a way to show you what He wants to say and how He wants to say it!

# Materials to Use
## Background

The background is the foundation for design elements that convey the message of the bulletin board. The most effective background materials complement the theme of the bulletin board or draw the viewer's attention to the message. The background should not compete for attention. For example, a bright red glossy paper is suitable for a joyous festival such as Christmas, while a humble fabric like burlap is more appropriate for the Lenten season.

Of all the materials that can be used successfully as bulletin board backgrounds, *paper* is probably the most common and most versatile.

*Bulletin board paper* in solid colors on large rolls is available from school supply companies. If your funds are limited and if you will make only a few bulletin board changes during the year, it is practical to begin with a single roll of white paper. As your needs expand, your selections will likely include red, blue, and green. These colors can provide necessary backgrounds throughout an entire church and school year.

*Construction paper* can also be used as a background. This works best on smaller areas (less than 30″ × 40″). When construction paper is used to cover large surfaces, the effect can be a bit patchy. Construction paper backgrounds are most effective when many elements will be mounted, thus covering many of the seams.

PAPER

*Gift-wrapping paper* makes an interesting background but must be chosen with care. When gift-wrap is used to cover an entire board, select a solid color or a design with a tiny pattern. The background should not be so busy or so bold that it overpowers the message to be displayed. Foil gift-wrap makes a good background, but if foil paper is used, the letters, borders, symbols, etc., should be limited to one color. White looks best on a background of red or green foil, while black looks best on silver or gold foil. Remember too that the lighting in relation to the position of the bulletin board can create a glare on a foil background. Be sure to take this into consideration.

*Wallpaper* provides an excellent background. Again, exercise care here so the background will not overpower the message. Subtle stripes and single-colored textures are best suited to add interest without detracting from the message. Prints may work if they are appropriate for the message of the bulletin board. When considering a print, it is best to choose those that depict things found in God's creation: trees, foliage, flowers, rocks, wood grain, and the like. Use only small prints with subtle coloring. Monochromatic color schemes (several shades and intensities of one color) can provide attractive backgrounds. Wallpaper can be expensive, but be on the lookout for special sales. For example, lumber companies, paint stores, hardware stores, or department stores often have promotional sales on single rolls or discontinued patterns. Sometimes these stores will even give away unsold rolls when sales end. And many stores are willing to donate such items for school or church purposes.

Materials other than paper can make effective and even dramatic bulletin board backgrounds. For instance, some kinds of *carpet* can be used as a bulletin board background. Solid colors work best. Short-napped flat surfaces are much easier to work with than shag or sculptured textures. Jute-backed carpets are easier to use than rubber-backed carpets. Carpet stores often sell remnants at very low cost or even give them away. Obviously, it is easier to find remnants for smaller bulletin boards than for larger ones. A hint for cutting shapes from carpet: transfer patterns to the back of carpet with chalk and carefully cut with a razor knife or utility knife. Mount carpet onto bulletin boards with long staples or strong pushpins.

*Fabrics* also make excellent backgrounds since they are readily available and can be used over and over without showing holes made by pins or staples. The same considerations given to paper choices apply to fabric choices. Fabric backgrounds are more effective if limited to solid colors or subtle textures, tiny prints, or nature prints.

A very wide range of fabrics is sold at discount stores, craft stores, and fabric stores, but don't be overwhelmed. Limit your search to woven fabrics, which work better than stretch fabrics since they retain their shape and aren't easily snagged.

When purchasing fabrics to be used for bulletin board backgrounds, remember that fabrics are sold by the yard or increments of the yard, such as one half or one fourth. Dressmaking fabrics like cotton and cotton blends are typically 45 inches wide. Craft and upholstery fabrics are usually 60 inches wide. Be sure to figure your bulletin board measurements accordingly. Fabric remnants (sometimes called "quarters" or "fat quarters") are generally not large enough for backgrounds but can be used for design elements on the bulletin board.

FABRIC

Woven *cotton* fabrics and cotton blends are ideal for bulletin board backgrounds because they are readily available, relatively inexpensive, and come in a rainbow of colors. Pastel colors that are usually not found in bulletin board paper are easy to find in woven cottons. Calico prints, such as those used for quilt making, may be suitable for some backgrounds. But again, care must be taken so the background does not compete with elements of the bulletin board that emphasize God's Word.

**Burlap** is an all-time favorite bulletin board background. Because of its coarse weave, burlap shows practically no wear even after years of use. (Fading might be the only problem.) It is available in a variety of colors, but burlap colors tend to be somewhat dark and drab. Be sure the color you select is appropriate for the message you wish to project.

**Felt** also makes a good bulletin board background. It is easy to work with, comes in a variety of basic colors, and is quite durable. But felt is generally quite expensive and stretches over time.

**Drapery and upholstery fabric** may be used for effective bulletin boards, however, they are usually more expensive than dressmaker fabrics. These fabrics come in a variety of weights, but they are generally heavier in weight. A disadvantage to heavier fabric is that it tends to droop or sag when spread across a large bulletin board. These fabrics are probably the least used as bulletin board backgrounds because of their weight and expense. However, clearance sales and garage sales may prove an economical source of lightweight drapery fabric.

Ready-made **sheets** are a good alternative to purchasing fabric by the yard. They come in an array of colors and patterns, and larger sheets provide for seam-free backgrounds if your bulletin board is large or long. Sales at department and discount stores are common.

The use of these basic background materials—paper, carpet, and fabric—is limited only by one's imagination. The same background cut for a specific bulletin board can serve in many ways. When combined with a variety of letters, borders, and symbols, it can take on a "whole new look."

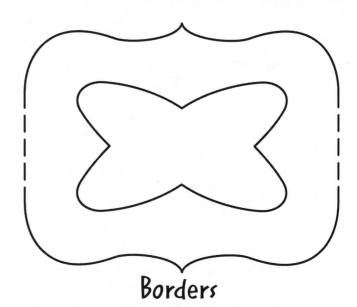

# Borders

For many people, a border is the finishing touch to a bulletin board. Effective border patterns are countless. School supply companies sell ready-made borders through stores and catalogs, but creating your own is not difficult as long as you follow some basic suggestions.

Borders should be compatible with the style of lettering and with the background design and color. For example, a geometric foil border on a burlap background with gothic letters would be incongruous; while a simply designed carpet border with block letters would be very harmonious with a burlap background. Borders and letters need not be the same color but they are usually more pleasing when cut from the same kind of material.

**Strip borders** are made by laying a pattern on fabric or paper, tracing lightly with pencil or chalk, and cutting.

Paper strip borders are the easiest and quickest to make since three or four strips of paper can be cut at once. Many kinds of paper can be used, just as for backgrounds. In fact, there is more freedom for using prints, stripes, etc., for borders than for backgrounds. Wallpaper and gift-wrap designs too bold for backgrounds may be just right for borders.

Fabric strip borders should be cut singly since layers of fabric tend to slip, thus making the

border uneven. The fabric chosen for borders could be heavier than fabric used for the background. Felt, drapery, and upholstery fabrics are especially good since they don't ravel, are easy to cut, and hold their shape without a lot of pins or staples. Since only long, narrow strips of fabric are required, drooping and sagging isn't usually a problem.

Borders made from carpeting are also very effective. However, if carpet is used, don't try a fancy border because it would be very hard to cut. Instead, cut a strip of carpet for each side of the bulletin board. While this is not a fancy border, it is interesting because the raised texture of the carpet creates a frame for the bulletin board.

To use the border patterns in this book most efficiently, transfer each pattern to a piece of poster board and then cut out the pattern. Then, as the need arises, the patterns will be ready to trace onto paper or fabric.

*Folded border patterns* may be made by folding paper accordion style, cutting a pattern along one side, and unfolding—just like cutting a string of paper dolls.

Construction paper is one of the best materials for a folded border, but gift-wrap, wallpaper, and other paper materials can also be used with great success. If the pattern selected for this style of border leaves open areas that create a see-through effect, solid colors should be used. Prints, stripes, or other designs tend to be to dis-

tracting when used with this type of border.

Some heavier fabrics like drapery and upholstery fabrics also lend themselves well to folded borders. Great care should be taken when folding and cutting to ensure an even border.

***Tips for making folded borders:***

Use one of the patterns in this book or create your own pattern.

Cut four strips of paper or fabric 1 ½" to 2" wide and as long as each side of the bulletin board. (If the material you wish to use is not long enough, cut several shorter pieces and splice them together as you pin the border to the bulletin board.)

Fold the strips accordion style to fit the pattern you have selected.

Cut as indicated on the pattern.

Open to reveal the connected pieces.

Pin or staple along edges of the bulletin board.

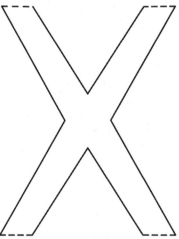

Several border patterns are included in this book beginning on page 53. Again, to make them durable and easy to use, transfer patterns to poster board and cut out so they are ready to use as they are needed.

**Single piece borders** are made up of individual pieces and are very effective, although they may be more time consuming to make and mount since they are cut out and then pinned or stapled one piece at a time. Materials suitable for borders may be found nearly everywhere. Consider the following:

Pine cones (thoroughly dried and free of pitch) are fine for harvest, Christmas, or winter themes.

Dried flowers work well for harvest themes. (Spray with hair spray after they are thoroughly dried to bring out the color.)

Silk flowers or greenery are especially effective for spring, Easter, and Trinity themes. Faded flowers can be covered with spray paint for a very striking border.

Many other household and classroom items may be used as borders as long as they are lightweight and thin enough to pin or staple to a bulletin board.

If desired, border pieces can be made easily from paper. Almost any shape can be used, but the shape must be in keeping with the theme of the bulletin board: lilies for Easter or spring; leaves for harvest or Trinity; stars for Christmas or Epiphany; poinsettias for Christmas; crosses for Lent, etc.

Several single-piece border patterns are included in this book beginning on page 53. On any given board, one pattern in a single color may be used or two or three complimentary colors and patterns may be combined. The pieces should be arranged symmetrically to create a finished look.

## Lettering

Lettering should always be compatible with the age of the viewer. For adults and older children, use all capitals in a decorative design. For younger children, use very simple capital and lowercase letters. There are many ready-made letter patterns marketed by a variety of companies.

The alphabet patterns on page 58 are suitable for various age groups. These letter patterns will be easiest to use if transferred to poster board and cut out. For efficient storage, cut strips of poster board and tape them inside a gift box to create a section for each letter or pair of letters. Label each section with a marker.

As with borders, letters may be cut from construction paper, gift-wrap, foil, felt, fabric, etc. If prints or other designs are used, it may be wise to outline each letter with a marker to ensure readability. Cutting two letters each of contrasting colors and gluing them together in a slightly offset manner can also create an interesting effect.

# How to Proceed

Once you have an idea, sketch a draft of it—complete with borders, captions, etc., then—

### Be flexible:

Try using several letter styles until one seems best.

Arrange the letters in a variety of ways until one seems most effective.

Try several border patterns until one seems to be most compatible with the other elements of the board.

Try using a variety of materials—not for a "sensational" effect, but to strive for the combination that best brings out God's message.

### Be precise:

Select a background and letter and border patterns that project sincerity (God's Word is not to be taken lightly).

Use colors which best stress the ideas being presented—

- ❀ Green for Christian growth
- ⊕ Blue for loyalty
- ❤ Red for salvation through the blood of Christ
- ☀ Yellow for Christ, the Light of the world
- ⚡ Purple for sin and transgression
- ❄ White for purity and righteousness

Use bold and dramatic colors and textures to present bold and dramatic ideas; use pastels and softer textures to present love, gentleness, etc.

Use symbols that are scripturally sound, even though they may not be "artistically correct." Make sure symbols project ideas rather then merely adding decorations. (After all, not everyone will read the caption; make sure they get the message at a glance.)

Do all cutting, painting, drawing, gluing, etc., with the greatest of care. Extra time taken on God's bulletin board is never wasted!

# The Final Touch

Once the last letter has been cut, the last pin put in place, and the last scrap picked up, there is but one thing left to do: thank the Lord for this opportunity to serve Him and pray that all who see His Word represented on your bulletin boards will receive the message of God's grace and mercy through Jesus, our Lord and Savior.

## God's blessings!

# Feed My Lambs

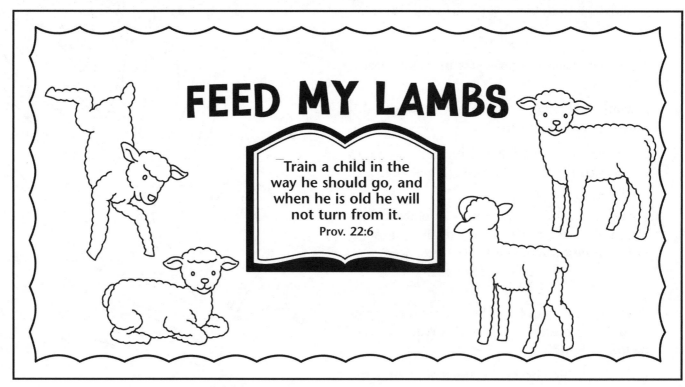

FEED MY LAMBS

Train a child in the way he should go, and when he is old he will not turn from it.
Prov. 22:6

This bulletin board is especially suitable for beginnings—the school year, the Sunday school year, or vacation Bible school. It is also ideal for a general theme of nurturing the young with the milk of God's Holy Word. With this in mind, it may be used for the installation of day school or Sunday school teachers, Sunday school superintendents, board of education members, etc.

The number of lambs can vary depending on the size of the bulletin board or whether it is intended for a specific class. For instance, if space allows, the name of each child may be written on a lamb that is posted on the bulletin board.

## Suggested Color Scheme

*Background:* red or blue bulletin board paper

*Border:* yellow calico print wrapping paper or fabric

*Letters:* black construction paper

*Lambs:* white, outlined with black marker

*Bible:* black cover with gold foil page edges and white open page (calligraphy would be very effective for the verse). See the "Open Bible" instructions on page 52 for help in constructing the Bible.

10

11

# Let Your Words in Me Take Root

This caption, taken from the hymn, "Speak, O Lord, Your Servant Listens," recognizes the true Source of all wisdom. The roots of the tree draw nourishment from the four Gospels.

This design is suitable for the beginning of the day school or Sunday school year, for a series of Bible classes, or for the Trinity season—our season of growth.

The tree can be used for other bulletin boards as well. For example, fruit of assorted shapes and sizes made from construction paper can be labeled with the fruits of the Spirit and attached to the tree. Or "Only God Can Make a Tree" can be used as a caption for a bulletin board with a creation theme.

## Suggested Color Scheme

**Background:** blue bulletin board paper

**Tree Top:** green carpet or fabric

**Tree Trunk:** brown carpet or fabric

**Letters:** brown construction paper

**Border:** green fabric leaves cut from patterns on these two pages

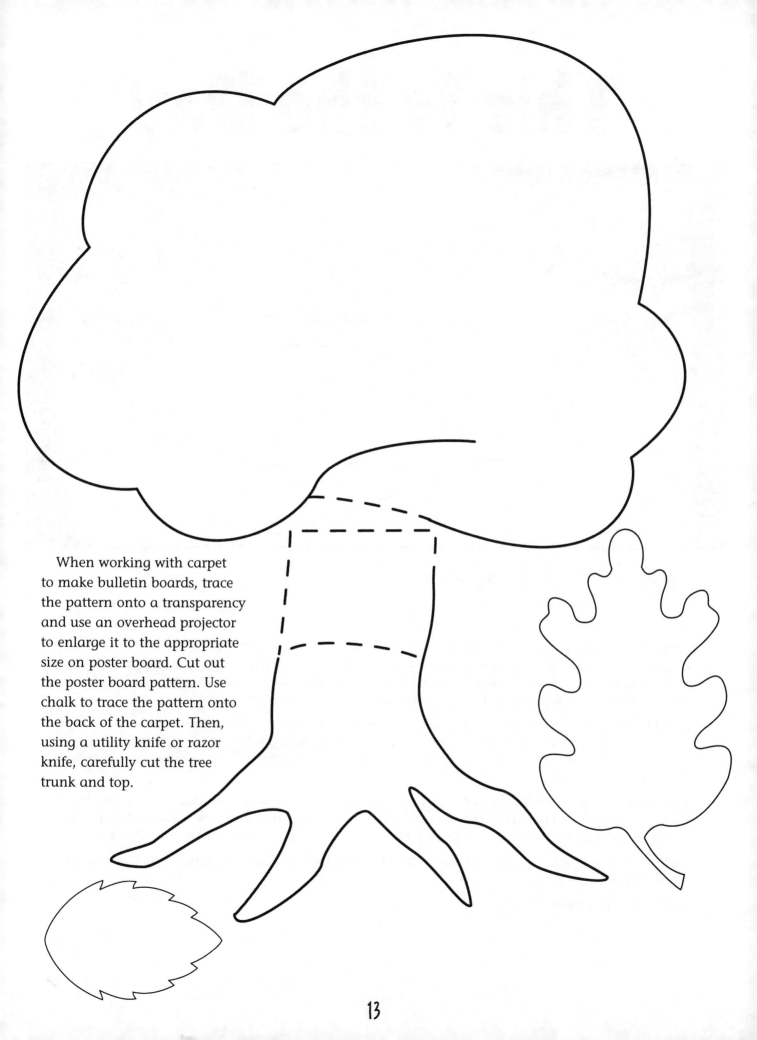

When working with carpet to make bulletin boards, trace the pattern onto a transparency and use an overhead projector to enlarge it to the appropriate size on poster board. Cut out the poster board pattern. Use chalk to trace the pattern onto the back of the carpet. Then, using a utility knife or razor knife, carefully cut the tree trunk and top.

# This Is the Day

THIS IS THE DAY
WHICH THE LORD
HAS MADE
I WILL REJOICE AND
BE GLAD IN IT."

## Suggested Color Scheme

**Background:** blue to indicate sky

**Trees:** black bulletin board paper. (This is easier to work with than piecing together several sheets of construction paper.) Cut two trees and reverse one to get a right and a left. For efficient storage, wrap trees around the cardboard core from a roll of gift-wrap. Depending on the size of the bulletin board, the branches at the top of each tree may be extended so they meet in the center.

**Hillsides:** green bulletin board paper, textured fabric, or carpet. No pattern should be required. Simply measure about one-third up the side of the bulletin board to get the height and cut shapes similar to those shown here. If you cut hillsides from paper or fabric, overlap shapes when pinning for a more realistic effect.

**Leaves:** yellow, gold, orange, red, green, and brown construction paper. See pages 12, 13, and 15 for patterns; the oak leaf pattern is best suited for this bulletin board because of its size and shape. But if this design is being adapted for a small bulletin board, consider using a smaller leaf pattern.

**Sun:** yellow construction paper. Use any round object of desired size as a pattern—paper plate, cover, pizza pan, etc.

**Letters:** black construction paper

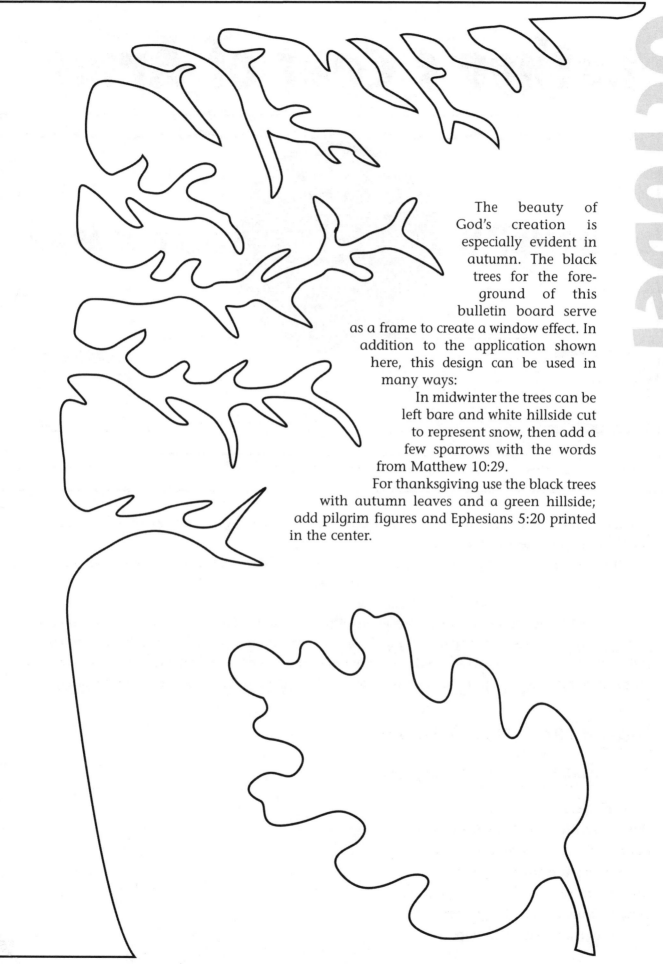

The beauty of God's creation is especially evident in autumn. The black trees for the fore-ground of this bulletin board serve as a frame to create a window effect. In addition to the application shown here, this design can be used in many ways:

In midwinter the trees can be left bare and white hillside cut to represent snow, then add a few sparrows with the words from Matthew 10:29.

For thanksgiving use the black trees with autumn leaves and a green hillside; add pilgrim figures and Ephesians 5:20 printed in the center.

# Luther's Coat of Arms

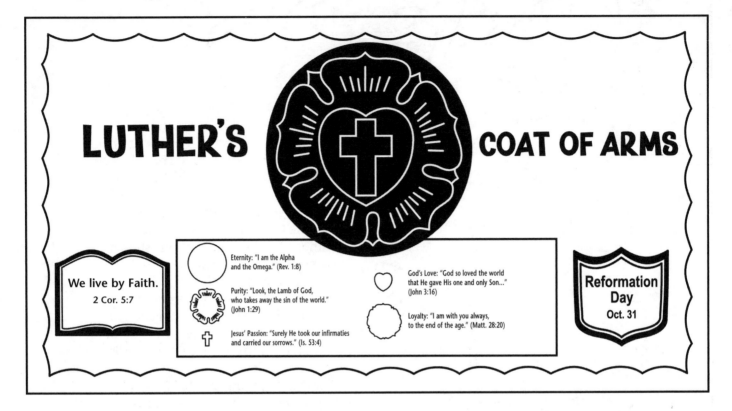

Reformation Day is an ideal time to create a bulletin board that offers an explanation of the symbolism used in Luther's coat of arms.

Luther's shield is shown in its entirety. The effect is best if each part is made separately and then glued together in layers. As you make the shield, be sure to cover it with books or other flat, heavy objects to prevent curling while it is drying.

The elements that make up Luther's shield are also shown individually with a description and a supporting Scripture verse. These smaller symbols may be drawn on a piece of poster board and colored with markers. Be sure to provide a sufficient amount of space (lines lightly penciled in) to allow for all the printing required. The printing should be done with a permanent marker to avoid smearing.

## Suggested Color Scheme

**Background:** blue bulletin board paper

**Luther's Seal:**

**Outer Circle:** gold foil mounted on poster board

**Heart:** red foil or construction paper

**Cross:** black construction paper

**Open Bible:** see instructions on page 52

**Border:** white construction paper

**Letters:** black construction paper

**Shield:**

*Outer Layer:* black construction paper
*Middle Layer:* gold foil
*Inner Layer:* white typing paper

Trace these patterns onto a transparency and enlarge them onto poster board to the desired size. You will need elements of the seal in two sizes: larger for the assembled seal and smaller for the description of each element.

# In Everything Give Thanks

This bulletin board design emphasizes how we can look to Scripture for strength and remember that Jesus is the Bread of life. Pilgrim silhouettes face the center with the open Bible between then. A shock of real wheat pinned behind the Bible is a symbol for the Bread of life. Look for wheat at craft stores, school supply stores or farmer's markets. You may also cut corn shocks from construction paper, as shown above, to place behind the open Bible instead of wheat.

## Suggested Color Scheme

**Background:** gold foil or yellow bulletin board paper

**Border:** black construction paper

**Letters:** black construction paper

**Silhouettes:** black construction paper. Use patterns provided here or use ready-made Pilgrim silhouettes.

**Open Bible:** see instructions on page 52 (gold foil pages may be omitted if a gold foil background is used.)

November

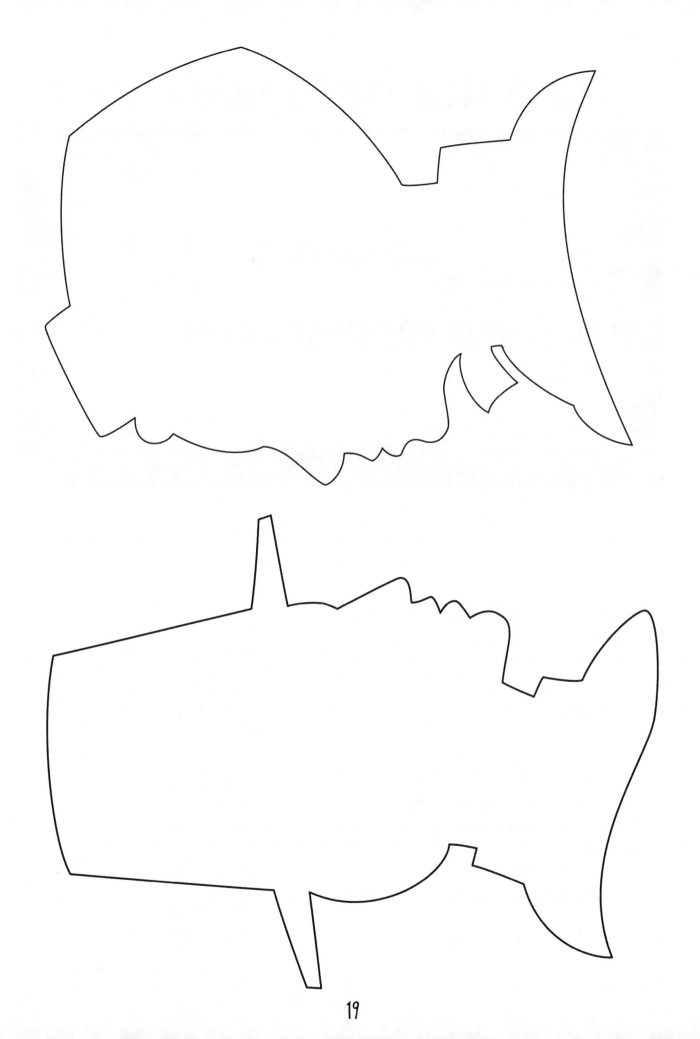

19

# Thank God for Promises Kept

The subtle rainbow in this bulletin board design symbolizes God's promises to His children. The black trees serve to frame the Gospel as conveyed in John 3:16. Each of the phrases is printed on a ribbonlike banner. Above the banner is a symbol for each phrase.

## Suggested Color Scheme

*Background:* light blue bulletin board paper on which a watercolor rainbow has been painted. Be sure to paint the rainbow while the paper is flat on a table or the floor to prevent the colors from running.

*Trees:* black construction paper (pattern on page 15)

*Border:* black construction paper (bottom only)

*Banners:* white construction paper

*Stable and Manger:* black construction paper with gold foil rays radiating from the infant's head

*Cross:* black construction paper

*Crown of Thorns:* brown construction paper

*Crown of Glory:* gold foil with sequins, rhinestones, etc.

*Crown of Thorns:* Make two crowns. Cut a slit in the middle. Then twist them together for a 3-D effect.

*Cross* is made with two strips of black construction paper; one should be cut to measure 1¼" x 14" and the other should be cut to measure 1¼" x 7".

*Banners:* cut from white construction paper; may need to be made larger or smaller than the pattern provided depending on the size of the bulletin board. This is easily done by extending the fold line.

21

# Peace on Earth

The dove of peace carries an olive branch as the Christmas message is proclaimed. This bulletin board provides an excellent opportunity to try creating your own stylized letters similar to those shown here. Otherwise, any of the letter patterns beginning on page 58 will work well. Your choice will depend only on the size of the bulletin board.

## Suggested Color Scheme

*Background:* royal blue bulletin board paper

*Border and Letters:* white construction paper

*Dove:* white paper. The farther wing and the body are pinned flat to the bulletin board. The wing on the outside of the body is slit and overlapped to create an "off-center cone shape." When pinned to the body in this way, the wing will stand out for a 3-D effect. White quilling paper may be used for the extended lines.

*Leaves:* green construction paper. Arrange the leaves along the stem with the largest at the bottom and the smallest at the top. Make several leaves of each size. Crease lengthwise and pin in center for a 3-D effect.

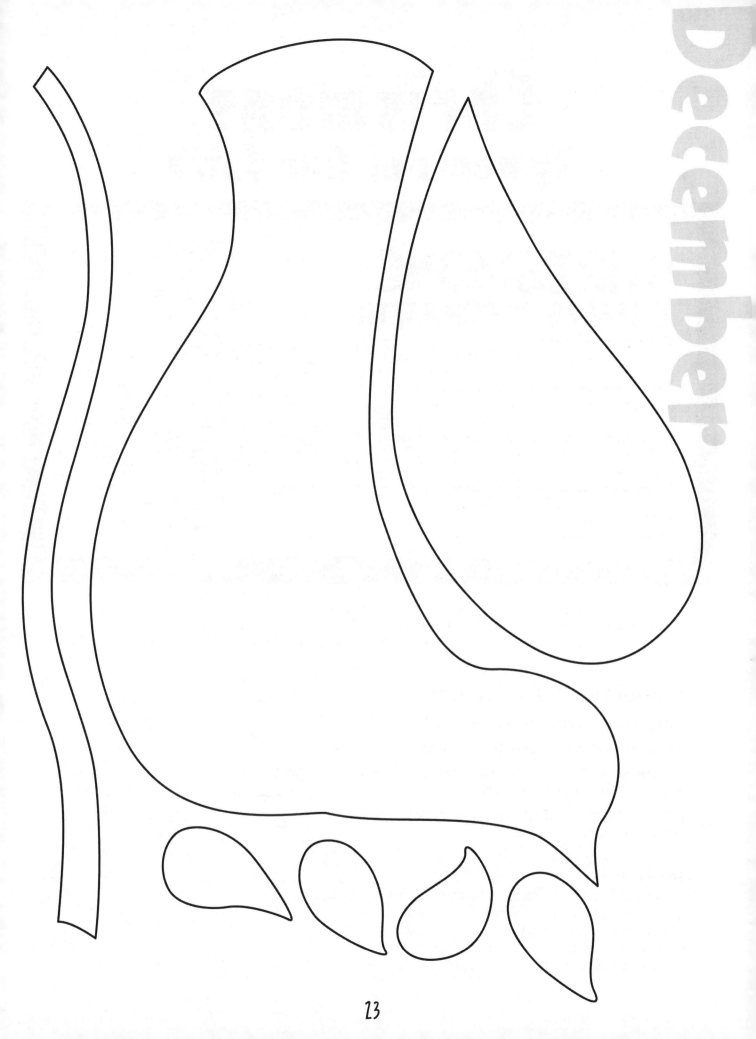

23

# Chrismons
## Symbols of Our Faith

This bulletin board is educational as well as inspirational.
Each Chrismon is shown in full size on the tree. It is then shown
again in miniature on a card that explains the meaning of the symbol.

## Suggested Color Scheme

**Background:** bright red bulletin board paper

**Border and Letters:** white construction paper

**Chrismons:** white poster board with gold foil and
gold glitter as indicated on each

**Tree:** green carpet (indoor-outdoor carpet is excellent)
or textured fabric

**Tree Pattern**

This pattern can be traced onto a transparency
and enlarged to desired size on poster board.
After pattern has been cut out, trace around it
with chalk onto the back of carpet. Carefully cut
out the tree using a utility knife or razor knife.

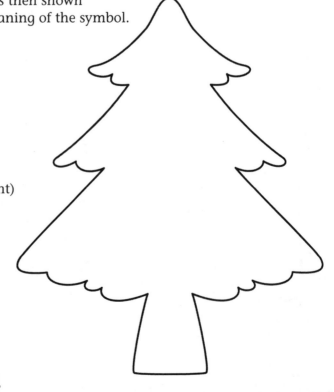

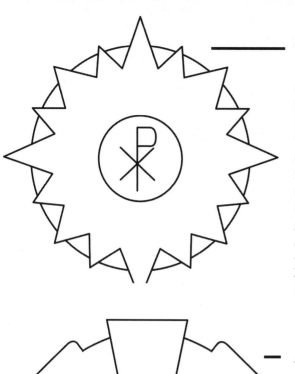

### The Chi Rho and the Sun

The letters *Chi* (X) and *Rho* (P) are the first two letters of Christ's name in Greek (*XPICTOC*—pronounced "Christos"). This symbol, an abbreviation of Christ's name, is one of the oldest and most familiar of all Christian symbols. The sun is a Messianic symbol of our Lord and recalls the prophecy in Malachi 4:2, where Jesus is called the "Sun of righteousness."

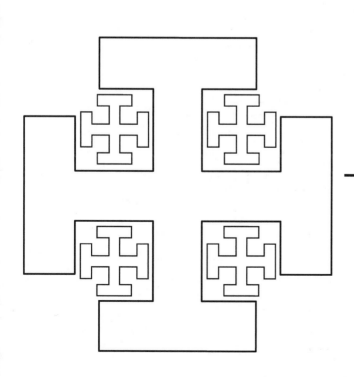

### A Cross Patee with Scrolls

The graceful outward curve of its arms is the hallmark of the Cross Patee. The cross combined with the circle of eternity and four scrolls represents the four evangelists— Matthew, Mark, Luke, and John—who reveal in their Gospels the story of God's plan of salvation for man.

### Christ—the Cornerstone

Christ is the Cornerstone of the church (Ephesians 2:20). Different forms of His name appear on each face of the stone.

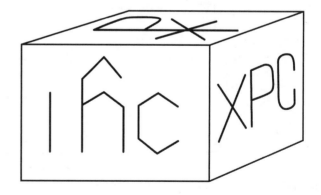

### The Jerusalem Cross

Crusaders emblazoned this cross on their shields. It is sometimes called the Fivefold Cross or the Crusader's Cross. The five crosses of this Chrismon symbolize the five wounds of our Lord. The four Tau crosses that comprise the large cross symbolize the Old Testament prophecies of the Savior. The four small crosses represent the spread of the Gospel to the four corners of the world.

25

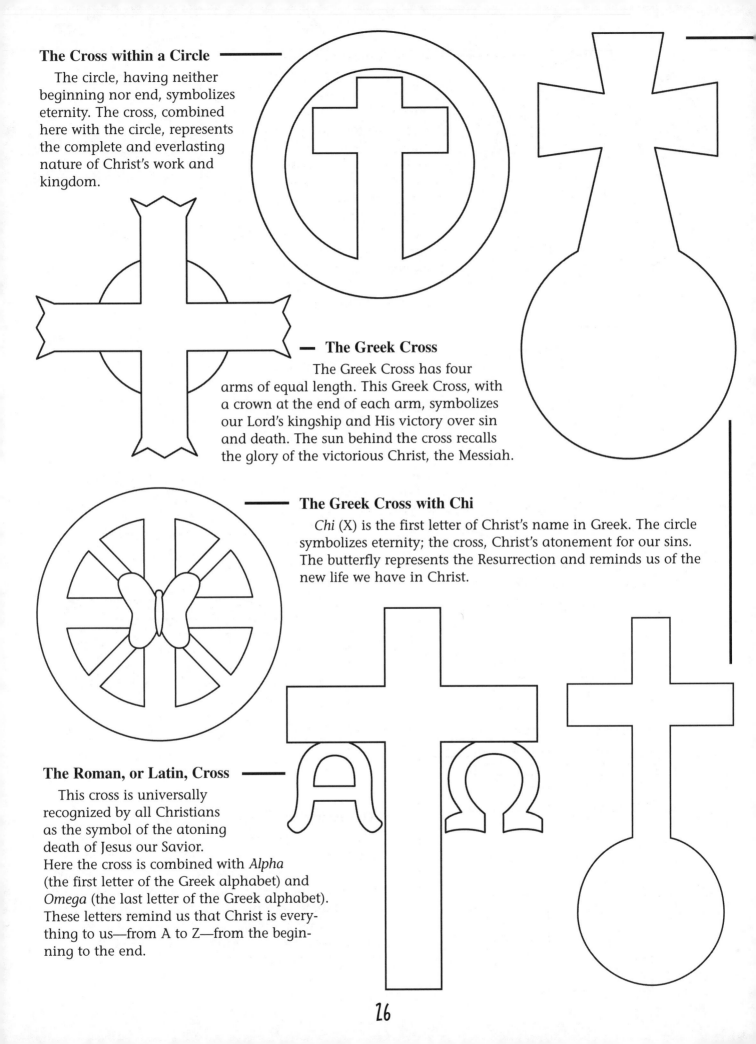

**The Cross within a Circle**

The circle, having neither beginning nor end, symbolizes eternity. The cross, combined here with the circle, represents the complete and everlasting nature of Christ's work and kingdom.

**The Greek Cross**

The Greek Cross has four arms of equal length. This Greek Cross, with a crown at the end of each arm, symbolizes our Lord's kingship and His victory over sin and death. The sun behind the cross recalls the glory of the victorious Christ, the Messiah.

**The Greek Cross with Chi**

*Chi* (X) is the first letter of Christ's name in Greek. The circle symbolizes eternity; the cross, Christ's atonement for our sins. The butterfly represents the Resurrection and reminds us of the new life we have in Christ.

**The Roman, or Latin, Cross**

This cross is universally recognized by all Christians as the symbol of the atoning death of Jesus our Savior. Here the cross is combined with *Alpha* (the first letter of the Greek alphabet) and *Omega* (the last letter of the Greek alphabet). These letters remind us that Christ is everything to us—from A to Z—from the beginning to the end.

## The Cross and the Sphere

This Chrismon is traditionally called the Cross of Triumph or the Cross of Victory. It is a symbol of the triumphant and glorified Lord. The sphere represents the entire world. The cross symbolizes Christ's triumph over the sin of the world.

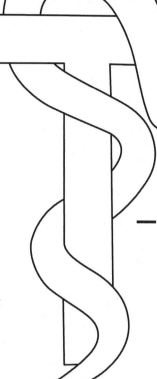

## Three Entwined Circles

Three perfect circles symbolize the eternal nature of the three persons in the Trinity and have long been a familiar way to express the doctrine of the Trinity.

The entwined circles show that there are three distinct Persons yet one eternal God.

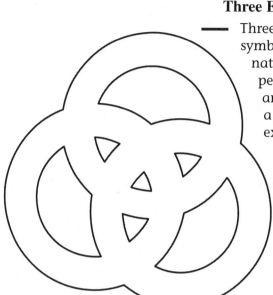

## The Tau Cross

This is a cross shaped like the Greek letter T, which is called *Tau*. This T-shaped cross is sometimes called the Old Testament Cross because it is said to have been the type of cross on which Moses placed the bronze snake (Numbers 21:8–9; John 3:14). In Christian art, the thieves crucified with Christ are often depicted on Tau crosses.

## IHC

This symbol is formed from the first three letters of the Greek word for Jesus, *IHCOYC*. A variation, IHS, is also used. Together with the cross, IHC and IHS remind us that our ransom from sin, death, and the devil was paid for by Christ's suffering and death on the cross.

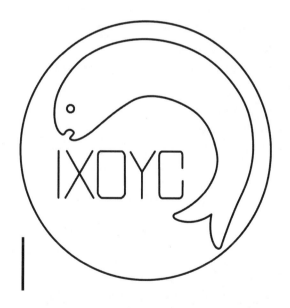

## IXOYC—Ichthus, or Fish

An acrostic used by early Christians. The letters *IXOYC* make up the Greek word for fish; they are also the first letters in Greek for "Jesus Christ, Son of God, Savior." This symbol was one of profound significance for the early Christian, testifying to eternal comfort and salvation found only in Jesus Christ.

# Every Morning Mercies New

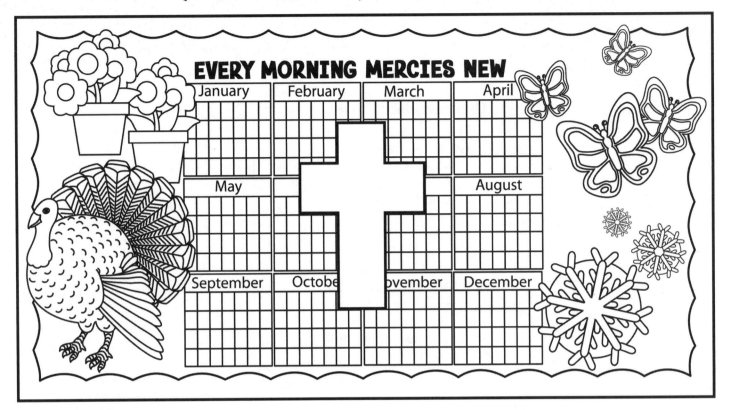

EVERY MORNING MERCIES NEW

| January | February | March | April |
|---|---|---|---|
| May | | | August |
| September | October | November | December |

The New Year is a wonderful time to remind children and adults alike that God daily forgives us and blesses our lives with a fresh, new opportunity to live for His glory! For this bulletin board design, a desk calendar, which has been taken apart and arranged in groups, indicates the four seasons of the calendar year. Symbols for each season represent our Father's earthly gifts to us. And the cross in the center is a reminder that it is through Jesus that we receive God's grace and mercy.

## Suggested Color Scheme

**Background:** light green or light blue bulletin board paper

**Border and Letters:** dark green, dark blue, or black construction paper

**Cross:** black with gold numbers or gold with black numbers

**Snowflakes:** white typing paper

**Butterflies, Flowers, Turkey:** white construction paper colored with markers

**Tree:** (optional) black construction paper

January

29

# Let the Spirit Lead You

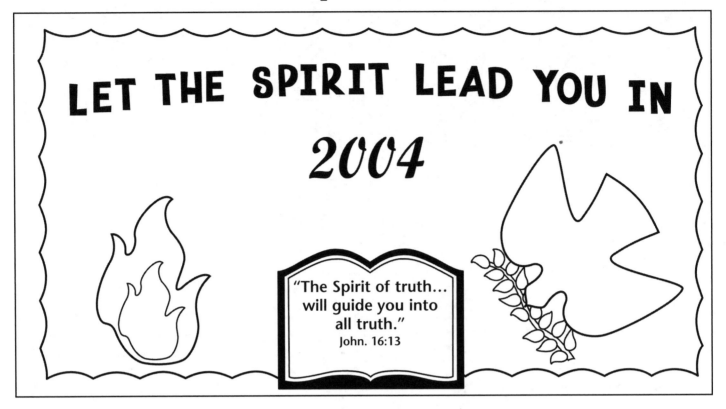

LET THE SPIRIT LEAD YOU IN 2004

"The Spirit of truth...
will guide you into
all truth."
John. 16:13

For Christians, the theme of every new year and every new beginning can be submission to the Holy Spirit's guidance. Use this bulletin board design to illustrate this theme when your school or Sunday school resumes after the new year. It can also be used for Pentecost, the opening of the school year, confirmation, or graduation.

## Suggested Color Scheme

*Background:* royal blue bulletin board paper or fabric

*Border and Letters:* white construction paper

*Flames:* red, orange, gold, and yellow construction paper

*Dove:* white construction paper

*Olive Branch:* dark green construction paper. See patterns on page 23. (For a 3-D effect, crease each leaf lengthwise and pin in the crease, and arrange along the stem.)

*Open Bible:* see instructions on page 52

*Tassel Bookmark:* (optional) braided red yarn with hanging tassel

January

31

# Love Is a Gift from God

Familiar "love" verses from Scripture remind Christians that all love has God as its source. We can love others only because God first loved us. Notice that in this design the words "Love Is a Gift from God" are displayed in larger letters. An observant viewer will note that this is a reversal of the universally known Scripture verse "God is love."

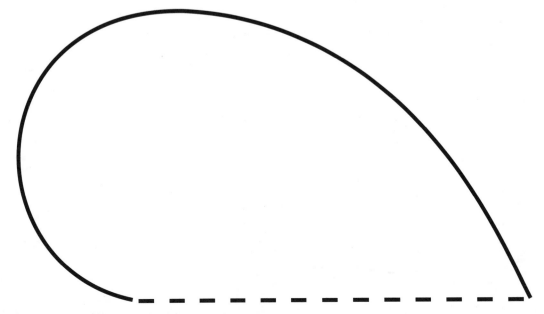

# Suggested Color Scheme

**Background:** white bulletin board paper

**Border and Letters:** red and gold patterned wallpaper or fabric

**Center Hearts:** white construction paper; print appropriate Bible verses on hearts

**Outer Hearts:** red ready-made heart-shaped lace doilies

**Note:** If you choose to use a red background instead, borders, letters, and lace hearts should be white. Borders and letters would then be effective if done in a white and gold patterned wallpaper or fabric.

# There Is But One Perfect Love

THERE IS BUT ONE PERFECT LOVE
THAT IS THE LOVE OUR FATHER HAS
FOR HIS CHILDREN

The single large heart shown for this bulletin board design symbolizes that God's love for His children is shown through Jesus. A black cross adorned with white flowers reminds us of Christ's death upon the cross and His glorious resurrection three days later.

## Suggested Color Scheme

**Background:** red bulletin board paper

**Border and Letters:** white construction paper

**Flowers:** white plastic or ready-made white silk flowers

**Cross:** black construction paper

**Hearts:** see pattern on next page

**Large outer heart:** white paper lace doilies cut in half and arranged in a scallop design

35

# For This Cause

"FOR THIS CAUSE CAME (HE) INTO THE WORLD.."
John 18:37 KJV

...THAT THE WORLD THROUGH HIM MIGHT BE SAVED.
John 3:17 KJV

This bulletin board clearly shows the direct connection between Christ's birth at Christmas and His death and resurrection at Easter. The infant's hands that reach toward the cross indicate the ultimate purpose of Christ's life on earth. The crown and earth represent Christ as Lord of lords and King of kings.

The entire scene can be traced onto a transparency and enlarged to the desired size by using an overhead projector. Then, watercolors can be used to paint the background onto white paper.

## Suggested Color Scheme

**Background:** white bulletin board paper or white poster board. Two to four sheets of poster board should be enough to cover most bulletin boards. Tape the sheets together carefully when tracing the pattern onto the poster board.

**Border and Letters:** purple construction paper

**Sky:** light blue watercolor around clouds

**Earth:** green to represent land and blue to represent water

**Crown:** gold foil

**Manger:** brown construction paper, white blanket, yellow straw

**Infant:** white paper colored with flesh-tone crayon and brown crayon for hair

**Jesus' Hands:** white paper colored with flesh-tone crayon

**Crown of Thorns:** brown construction paper or white paper colored with brown marker

**Cross:** brown construction paper with wood grain added with black marker.

**Rays of sunlight:** yellow watercolor blended into light blue sky

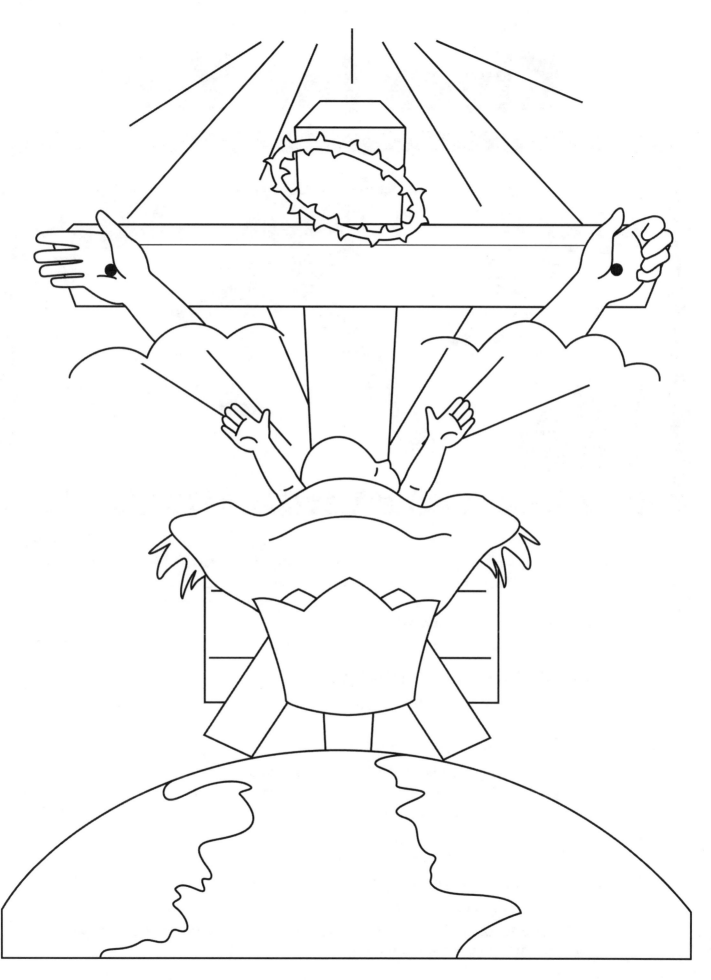

37

# Given for You

The tiny drops of red blood are the focal point of this display. Although simple in design, this bulletin board inspires serious reflection on the meaning of Christ's death on the cross for everyone. While this theme is most appropriate during the Lenten season and Holy Week, it is also very fitting anytime and anywhere the Lord's Supper is celebrated. The clusters of grapes reinforce the concept of the real presence of Jesus' body and blood in the bread and wine.

## Suggested Color Scheme

*Background:* white bulletin board paper (off-white wallpaper or fabric with a very subtle design is also very effective)

*Border and Letters:* purple construction paper

*Cross:* black construction paper cut 3″ or 4″ wide and as long as appropriate for the size of bulletin board used

*Crown of Thorns:* brown construction paper

*Cluster of Grapes:* white construction paper colored with markers and covered with clear contact paper for a glossy effect

*Leaves:* green construction paper creased in the center for a 3-D effect

*Vine:* brown yarn coiled here and there as needed to fill in spaces between leaves

*Chalice and Paten:* gold foil; purple construction paper for wine in the chalice; white or ivory construction paper for communion wafers in the paten

## Construction tips and suggestions:

✝ See pattern on page 21. Cut one crown in a continuous oval. Cut a second and slit as marked. Twist the crown with the slit around the solid crown for a 3-D effect.

✝ Cut one chalice from gold foil and glue to construction paper backing for added strength. Cut construction paper backing away from gold chalice. Slit along line. Cut "blood-wine" for chalice from red construction paper or red foil and insert into slit in gold chalice.

✝ Cut several drops of red from construction paper.

✝ Cut five to seven wafers from construction paper. Or use Styrofoam or craft foam wafers.

✝ Cut one paten from gold foil, glue to construction paper backing, and cut away backing paper. Slit along line and insert wafers.

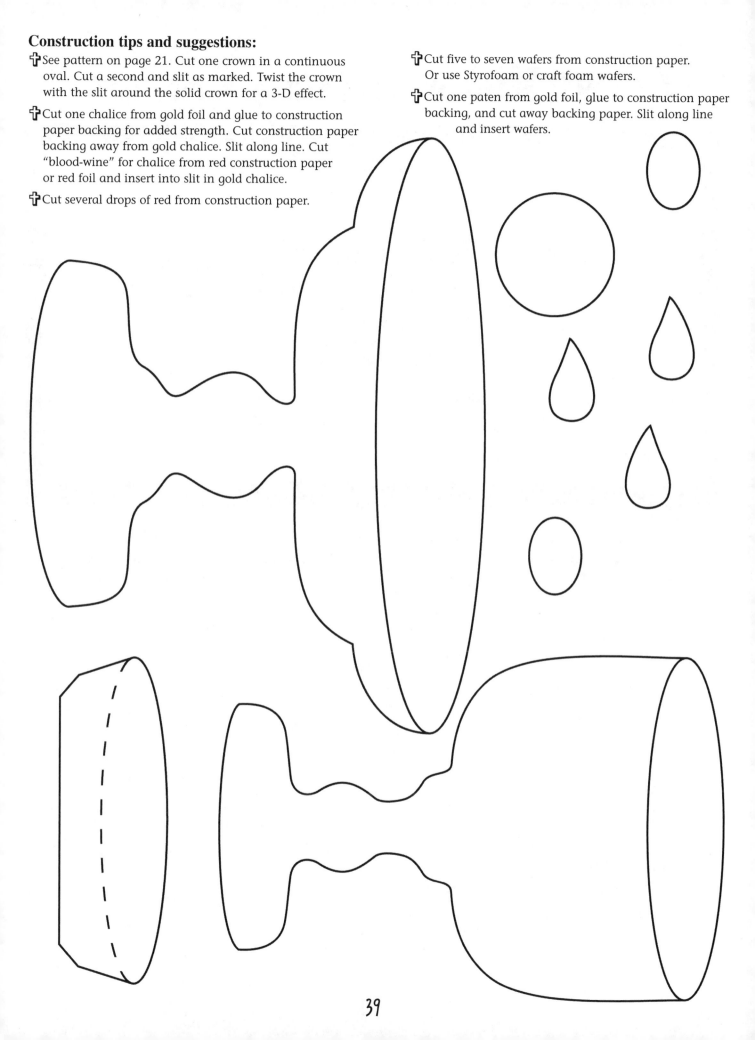

39

# Crown Him with Many Crowns

CROWN HIM WITH
MANY CROWNS
FOR HE IS
LORD OF ALL

This well-known Easter anthem reminds us of Christ's victory over sin, death, and the devil and encourages us to always remember that it is through His death and resurrection that Jesus won for us the gift of eternal life. This bulletin board design lends itself to Palm Sunday and the Easter season. It may be used for Christ the King Sunday.

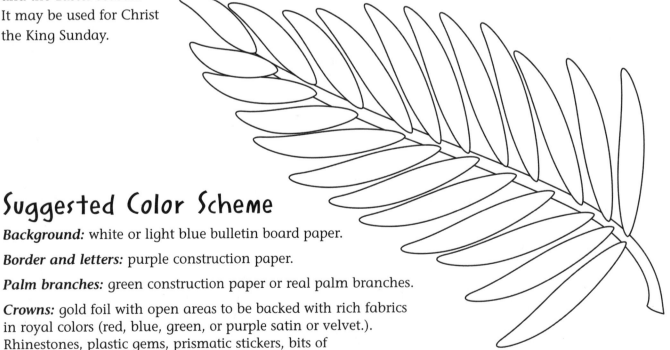

## Suggested Color Scheme

*Background:* white or light blue bulletin board paper.

*Border and letters:* purple construction paper.

*Palm branches:* green construction paper or real palm branches.

*Crowns:* gold foil with open areas to be backed with rich fabrics in royal colors (red, blue, green, or purple satin or velvet.). Rhinestones, plastic gems, prismatic stickers, bits of costume jewelry may be used to trim the crowns.

# Because I Live

**BECAUSE I LIVE
YOU SHALL LIVE ALSO**
John 14:19

The cross, traditional symbol of Christ's sacrifice on our behalf, is further enhanced by the brilliant yellow sunrise that creates the background of this bulletin board. The rays of the sun extend to the perimeter of the display area and symbolize the spread of the Good News of salvation throughout the world. The flowers emphasize the message of new life in Christ.

## Suggested Color Scheme

*Background:* white bulletin board paper

*Border:* yellow construction paper or wide floral ribbon

*Letters:* black construction paper

*Sunrise:* yellow construction paper, preferably a shade or two darker than the letters and border

*Sun rays:* yellow construction paper or ribbon cut in varying widths and lengths

*Cross:* brown construction paper, woodgrain wallpaper, or very narrow strips of paneling

*Flowers:* construction paper or silk Easter lilies

# Come, Holy Spirit

COME HOLY SPIRIT

O Holy Spirit, omnipresent, free, I bring the only thing I really have - an empty vessel to be filled by Thee.

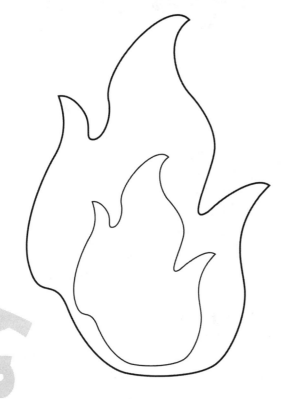

The coming of the Holy Spirit at Pentecost inspires awe in every Christian. This bulletin board serves as an invitation to the Holy Spirit to fill our empty vessels. This design is intended for display at Pentecost, but it would be an effective message to use at Baptisms, confirmations, and ordinations.

## Suggested Color Scheme

*Background:* royal blue or dark blue bulletin board paper

*Border and Letters:* white construction paper outlined with black or royal blue marker

*Dove:* white construction paper

*Flames:* red and orange construction paper

*Heart:* red construction paper

May

44

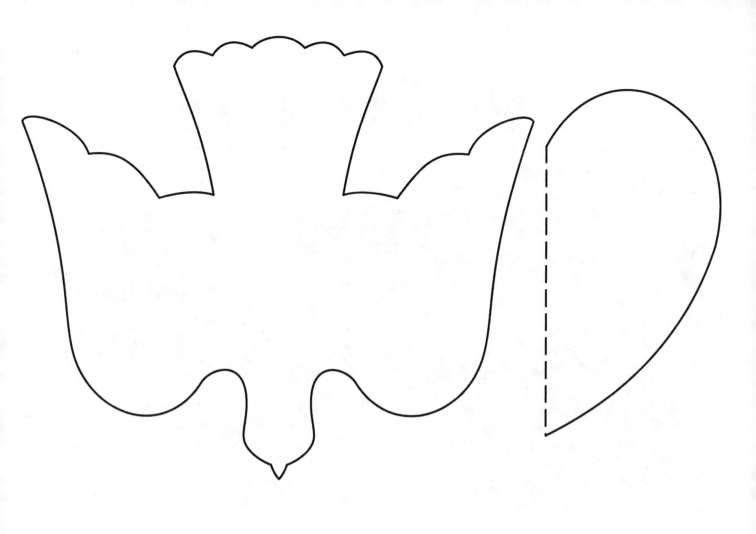

## Construction tips and suggestions:

- ❧ To add interest to the symbols shown, cut yarn of appropriate colors into ¼″ pieces. Use red for the heart; red, orange, and gold for the flames; white for the dove. Metallic or iridescent yarns are especially appealing.

- ❧ Using a paintbrush and white glue, coat the symbols with glue. Next, press the yarn onto the wet glue until the entire surface of symbol is covered with yarn. Pat yarn so it adheres. Work with one symbol at a time so glue does not dry too quickly.

- ❧ Allow glue to dry completely before attaching shapes to the bulletin board.

# Praise God

The triune God is indeed to be praised! This bulletin board is especially effective during the Trinity season of the church year and for Trinity Sunday, but it is appropriate to use when the students in your class or school are learning about Baptism as well. The triangle is a universal symbol for the Trinity. This concept is somewhat broadened by using names "Creator, Redeemer, and Comforter" rather than the more familiar "Father, Son, and Holy Spirit." One symbol is shown to represent each person of the Trinity, thus reminding the viewer of the unique work of the Father, the Son, and the Holy Spirit.

## Suggested Color Scheme

*Background:* royal blue bulletin board paper

*Border:* white construction paper

*Letters:* white and black construction paper

*Triangle:* white construction paper cut in strips 1¼" wide and of an appropriate length to form a triangle suitable for the size of the bulletin board

*Dove:* white construction paper

*Hand:* peach construction paper or white construction paper outlined in black marker and colored with flesh-colored crayons

*Cross:* gold foil

# God Gives Us New Beginnings

The cross is the focal point of this graduation theme, just as it is our focal point in life. At graduation time, we often hold up the individual student or the class as a whole and celebrate their passage to another chapter in their lives. However, this theme gives all glory and honor to God for His gift of new life through Jesus. The usual graduation symbols —the mortarboard and the diploma—are given a new meaning when combined with the rose, a symbol of God's creation; the cross, a symbol of Christ's work of salvation; and the dove and flame, symbols of the Holy Spirit's power in our lives.

# Suggested Color Scheme

**Background:** white bulletin board paper

**Border and Letters:** royal blue construction paper

**Mortarboard and Bible:** black (optional: use school colors or class colors for the mortarboard)

**Flame:** red, orange, and gold construction paper

**Dove:** white construction paper

**Cross:** gold foil, use pattern on page 47

**Diploma:** off-white paper rolled and tied with narrow ribbon

**Rose:** red construction paper for the flower, green for the leaves and stem

## Construction tips and suggestions:

✝ Use a parchment-type paper for the diploma and tie with black ribbon or with metallic yarn. To maintain a 3-D look, staple the diploma to the bulletin board.

✝ Use a silk rose or a rosebud and cut petals from green construction paper. Crease each leaf lengthwise and staple in the middle for a 3-D effect.

✝ Make tassel of matching or contrasting yarn and pin to center of mortarboard.

# Be Thou Our Guide

The Word of the Lord is at the heart of this graduation theme. Graduation is depicted here as a beginning of life for which God's guidance is both requested and accepted. The mortarboard and diploma symbolize commencement to a new phase of life, and the olive branches symbolize God's promises of peace and new life with Him. If bulletin board space allows, include Psalm 25:4–5. These verses would be especially effective if hand-lettered or rendered in calligraphy.

## Suggested Color Scheme

**Background:** white bulletin board paper

**Border and Letters:** royal blue construction paper or the color of the graduating class

**Mortarboard:** black construction paper, tassel may be made from white yarn or yarn in class colors

**Diploma:** white construction paper outlined with class colors; ribbon around diploma and tassel in black or class colors

**Open Bible:** see pattern on page 52

**Cross:** cross may be cut from gold foil or a wall cross may be used

**Olive Branch:** green construction paper

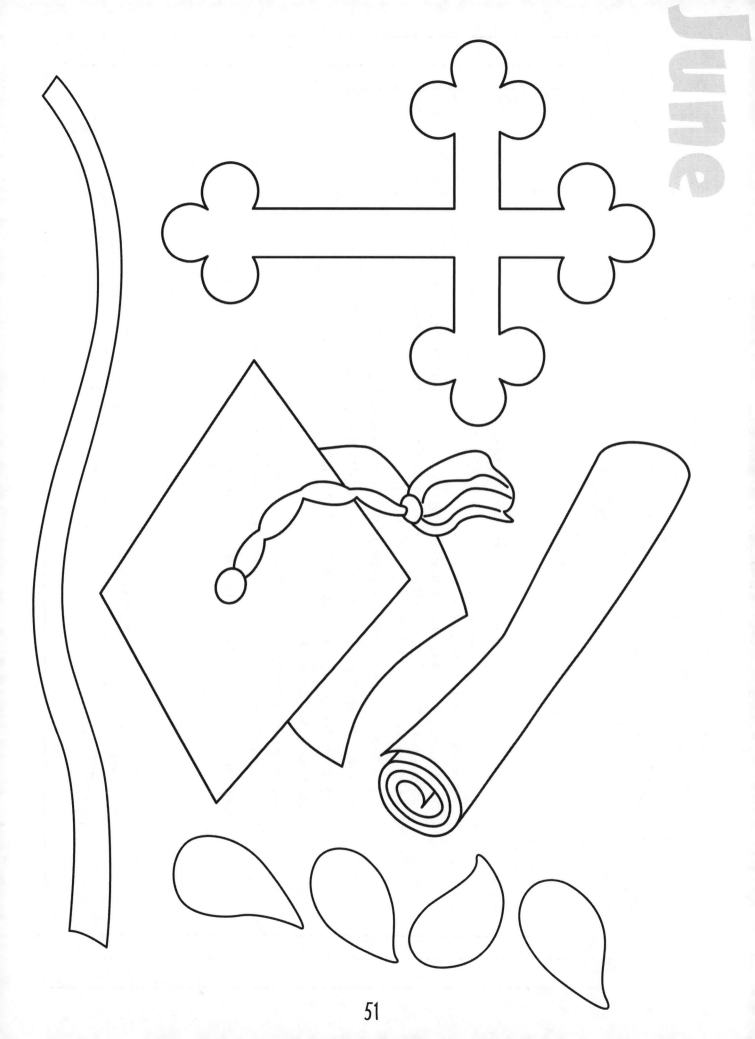

# Open Bible

The open Bible is often used in this collection of bulletin board ideas. Follow these easy steps to create your own pattern in the proper size.

1. Decide on the finished size for the Bible you will place on your bulletin board. For the pattern, cut a piece of paper a bit larger than the finished size. Fold it in half and draw a pattern similar to the one shown here.

2. Lay pattern on black construction paper and cut on all sides except the fold.

3. Recut the pattern slightly smaller ($\frac{1}{2}$"–$1\frac{1}{2}$" smaller, depending on the size of the Bible.)

4. Lay the smaller pattern on bright red or gold foil paper and cut as above.

5. Then, recut pattern smaller still.

6. Lay the smallest pattern on white paper and cut as above.

7. Use a ruler to mark light lines for printing, and print the selected verse.

8. Lay the three pieces as shown, and pin in the center to create an open book effect.

# Borders

Any one or a combination of these flowers may be used alone or with the leaf patterns shown on pages 12 and 13. (For a 3-D effect, crease each leaf lengthwise and pin in the crease.)

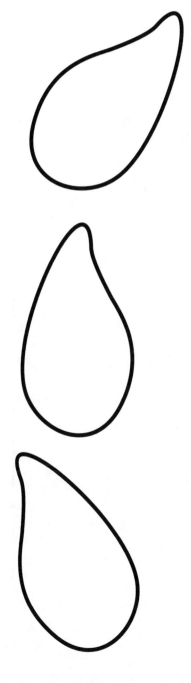

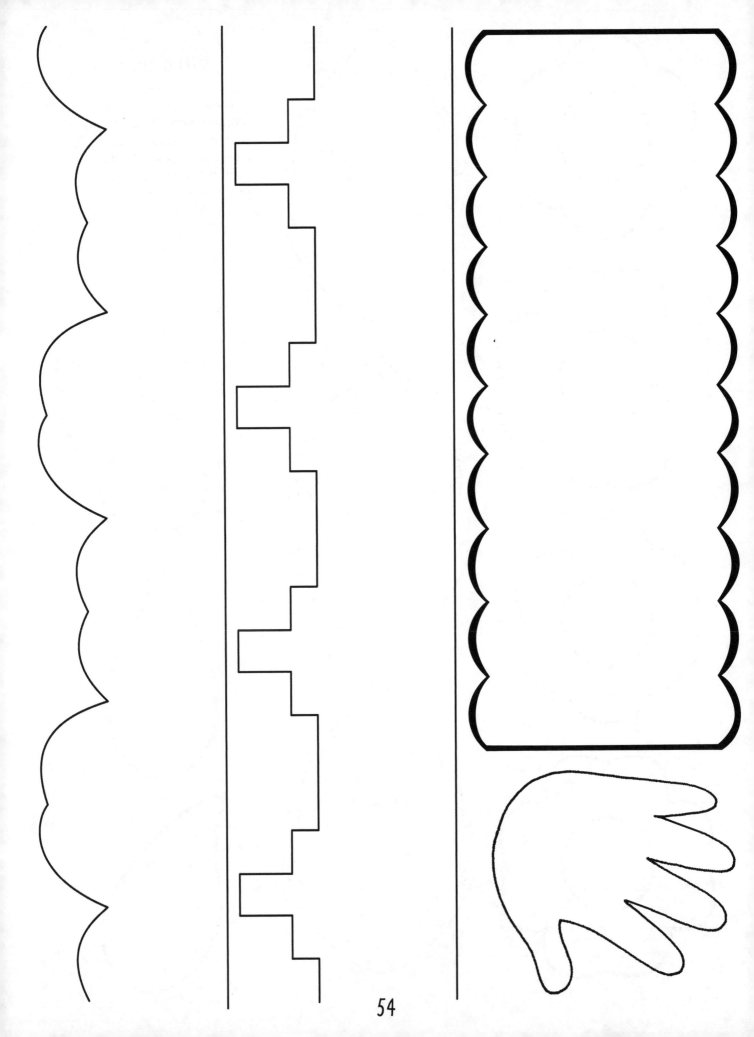

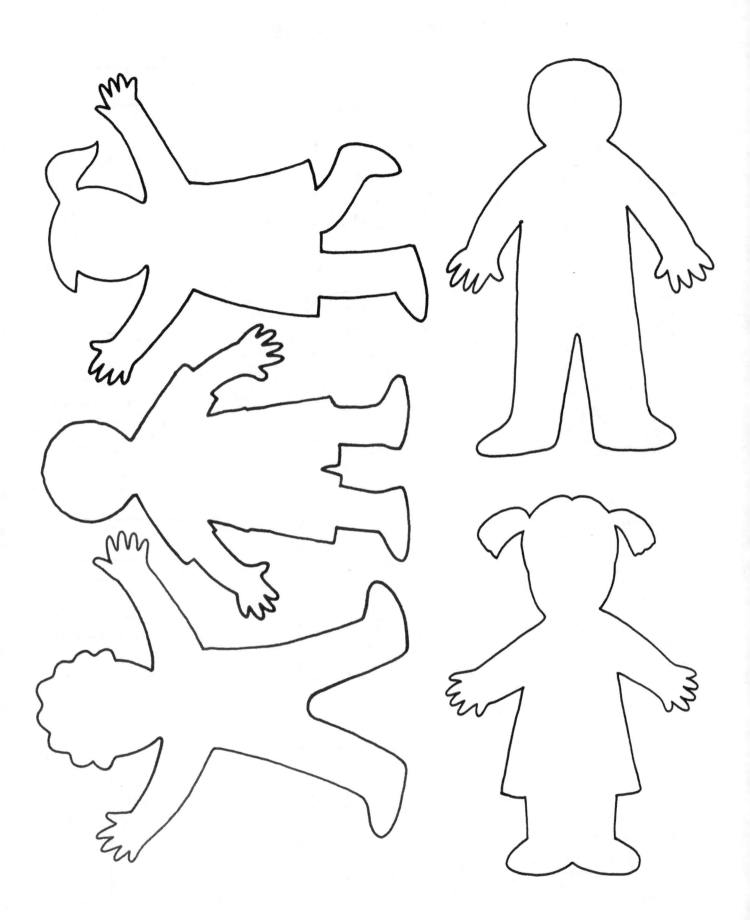

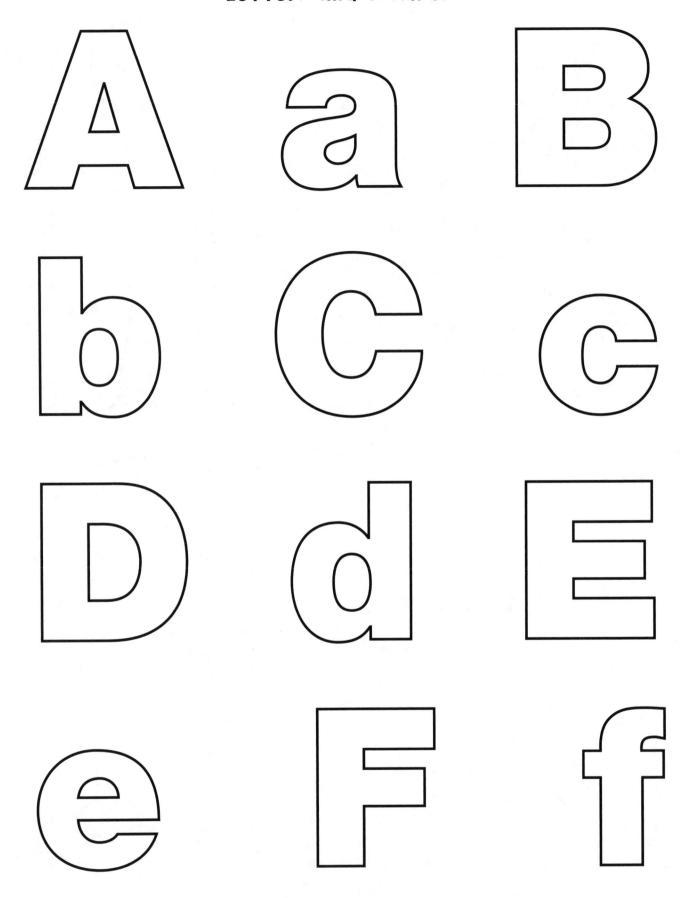

G g H

h l i J j

K k L l

M m N

n o o

P p Q

q R r

S s T

t U u V

v W w

X x Y y

Z z . ,

? ! & 1

2 3 4

5 6 7

8 9 0

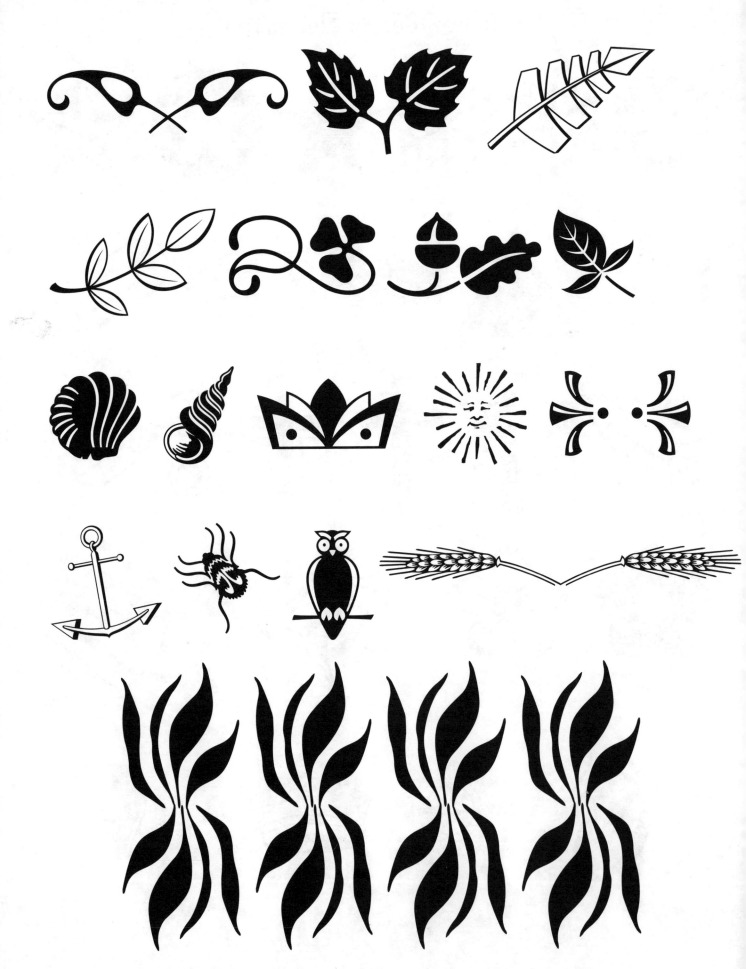